AROUND
DIDCOT
AND
THE HAGBOURNES
IN OLD PHOTOGRAPHS

To Amy on her birthday – a special occasion

AROUND
DIDCOT
AND
THE HAGBOURNES
IN OLD PHOTOGRAPHS

COMPILED BY
BRIAN LINGHAM

Budding
BOOKS

A Budding Book

First published in 1990 by Alan Sutton Publishing Limited

This edition published in 1998 by Budding Books,
an imprint of Sutton Publishing Limited
Phoenix Mill · Thrupp · Stroud · Gloucestershire GL5 2BU

A catalogue record for this book is available from the British Library

ISBN 1-84015-026-2

Typesetting and origination by
Sutton Publishing Limited.
Printed in Great Britain by
WBC Limited, Bridgend, Mid-Glamorgan.

CONTENTS

INTRODUCTION

Nowadays, it is strange to think that Didcot, a medium-sized modern town in south Oxfordshire, was once the smallest village in this area; smaller by far than Harwell, East Hagbourne, Blewbury or even Upton. Just how small Didcot was before the arrival of the railway in 1839, can be judged from the population figures given in the census of 1841: Harwell 857; East and West Hagbourne 814; Blewbury 443; South Moreton 417; North Moreton 397; Aston Tirrold 343; Upton 284; and, finally, Didcot at 203.

The opening of the railway station in 1844 determined that Didcot would grow — even if it was not until the next century. The station meant jobs, new people and a pressing housing demand. From the late 1860s onwards, this housing demand was to be met by the building of a new village, sited not in Didcot, but to the south-east in the parish of East Hagbourne. Its architect was Stephen Dixon of Parsonage Farm, East Hagbourne, and its name was Didcot Newtown or North Hagbourne — but this name was soon corrupted to Northbourne.

Before 1915, Didcot village or Old Didcot was still linked culturally and historically to the other villages in the area, where in each parish agriculture was the common link as it had been for centuries. Then there was the human link with members of the same families of all social classes living in more than one village. It was these links that bound the villagers together in a joint dislike of the newcomers of Newton. Nowhere was this feeling as strong as it was in Old Didcot. The railwaymen were not wanted and ignored if possible; as was Newtown which was regarded as an ugly intrusion of the town into the countryside.

The next surge in Didcot's history came with the arrival of the Army in 1915, and the establishment of Didcot Arsenal. It was the presence of the railway and its links north, south, east and west which determined that the Army should move part of the Woolwich Arsenal away from danger of enemy action during the First World War. Thus it was the Army and the Arsenal with its insatiable demand for labour, that was responsible for the rapid growth of Didcot during those inter-war years. This growth has never ceased – to the fear of its neighbours; at present Didcot's population is 16,000 plus and there is still no end in sight.

It could be argued that in comparison to Didcot's dramatic history, one full of change, the histories of the villages featured in this book have been relatively uneventful. The only traumas that might have occurred were rare and isolated. Theirs was a history of slow evolution, as season followed season. However, the villages, including Old Didcot, do (or did) share a common history, one that is linked primarily to the ownership of land and its use.

Most were established in Romano-British or Saxon times. Oddly enough, Old Didcot is probably one of the oldest settlements in the area, dating at around 200 BC to 600 BC. The settlement on Blewburton Hill is equally old. The evidence for Didcot's antiquity was found during a dig at All Saints' Rectory in 1982, when what was thought to be the foundation of an iron-age hut of those dates was uncovered. Iron-age pottery was also found. This is not so unreasonable as might be imagined because the site of Old Didcot was the best in the immediate area; positioned on a well-watered ridge, with rich farming land to the west and south, and well above the marshy low-lying ground to the east and south-east. Even today, this area is criss-crossed with streams, which are insignificant when compared to the virtual rivers that they would have been in former times.

All parishes, then Saxon estates (many were owned by King Harold), were feudalized after the Norman Conquest and the resulting fiefs or manors did, in some cases, have illustrious owners in the Middle Ages. Henry I owned both Blewbury (the Great Manor) and East Hagbourne; these he gave to two great religious houses, Reading and Cirencester abbeys. These monastic houses held the manors up to the Dissolution. At Harwell, Bishops Manor, Princes Manor and Baylliol or Brounz's Manor were named after their former owners: the Bishops of Winchester, Edward, the Black Prince, and the Brounz family. The latter was prominent in this area during the fourteenth and fifteenth centuries; owning land at Didcot and Sutton Courtenay as well as at Harwell. The manor of Didcot was owned by the Stonor family of Stonor Park, near Henley. At West Hagbourne, the manor was in the hands of the De Windsor family.

Interestingly, the De Windsor manorial complex at West Hagbourne was fortified: a survey of the manor made during the tenure of Clarice de Wyndesore (she must be the same Clarice who in 1403 is commemorated by a plaque in East Hagbourne church) suggests that the manor house was set within some form of fortified enclosure. The survey, of 1368, refers to: '... all houses from the said chamber to the Great Gate towards the north ... the kitchen, bake houses with well, the dovecot, the pond by the Great Gate ...'. The pond is obviously the same as that which is still in the centre of West Hagbourne. Beside it today, to the east, is the drive that runs from the road into Manor Farm. So the modern Manor Farm must occupy the same site – a centuries-long occupation – as that of Clarice de

Wyndsore's mid-thirteenth century manor. All that has gone besides the buildings, are the fortifications. There were also moated sites at East Hagbourne and South Moreton.

The Black Death of 1349 was a momentous event; one that was to have a tremendous effect on the economic and social life of the kingdom. It is difficult to measure its impact on this area due to a lack of documentary evidence, but what does exist suggests that every village suffered badly. There is an inquisition post-mortem for South Moreton, which states that 'the manor, including land . . . is uncultivated which used to be held by bondsmen and cottars who died in this pestilence'. This record could be misleading because it might be assumed that every village suffered in a like manner but this is not necessarily so. The Moretons do seem to have been unhealthy places to live in earlier centuries. The two villages, when first established, were sited in a great marsh that stretched from Sutton Courtenay and Didcot in the north, through the north-east corner of East Hagbourne below Hadden Hill, and then to and just beyond the Moretons. The place name Moreton does mean 'farm in the marsh'; and similar names in the other parishes attest to its former presence: Sutton Moor, Didcot Marsh, and East Hagbourne Marsh. Moor Ditch, which runs through north Didcot and Long Wittenham, a stream canalized by the Romano-British, was the first attempt to drain this marsh. The Moretons had another visitation of the Plague in 1603 (one of the great plague years), when North Moreton lost fifty-three inhabitants. No other local village was affected. Neither were they, nor were the Moretons, during the Great Plague of 1665.

The period of the Civil War of the seventeenth century was another highly traumatic episode in the histories of the villages; for not only was there constant plundering, the usual pillage and rape, by soldiers from both sides who were forced to live off the land, there was also the scourge of highly infectious disease brought into the villages by the same soldiers. It was probably typhus; for every village suffered on average a higher number of deaths than was usual. Once again, the Moretons suffered the most with fifty-three deaths in 1642/3.

The late Middle Ages saw an upsurge in house building, mainly timber-framed, which was carried through into the sixteenth and seventeenth centuries; a result of increased prosperity, especially during the Tudor period. We now enjoy the fruits of that prosperity centuries later in the picturesque villages that were essentially created then. Blewbury and East Hagbourne are fine examples, as are all the villages in this group. Each village is full of seventeenth-century (and even some of the late sixteenth) timber-framed houses, graded I or II. The earliest houses in the area are to be found at Harwell: Middle Farm or Baylliol or Brounz's Manor, dates from c. 1280; Wellshead Farm c. 1300; Prince's Manor c. 1500; and several cruck cottages, all dating from c. 1400.

After c. 1660, timber was gradually replaced by brick as a building material; though brick houses of the eighteenth and nineteenth centuries (other than at Harwell) are comparatively rare when compared to the numbers of earlier timber houses. This apparent anomaly has more to do with a changing economic climate as land became concentrated in fewer hands; and these tended to be those of absentee landlords. Coupled with this was an increase in the agricultural working class. Thus, the landlords saw no reason to replace these earlier houses with brick cottages; this is why there are so many still standing. Furthermore, when there are population increases, as during the eighteenth century, the landlords responded to these pressures by dividing up houses, which had formerly housed just one family, into two or three tenements.

But large brick houses, formerly farmhouses, are to be found in every village, at Harwell and East Hagbourne especially; the great fires at these villages are partly responsible for these. But the finest house in the district is to be found at Aston Tirrold, namely the very lovely Queen Anne period Manor House. Then there is the Malthus Schoolhouse of 1709 at Blewbury, and the partly early eighteenth-century Parsonage Farm of East Hagbourne.

Thatched timber houses with open fires are particularly prone to fire. Over the centuries this area has seen three disastrous fires: at East Hagbourne in 1659; Harwell in 1852, and Upton in 1934. The East Hagbourne fire broke out on 10 March 1659; and, apparently, before it was under control, almost every house in the village had burnt down. The suffering was so great that Charles II issued a proclamation in 1661 drawing attention to the 'great impoverishment and deplorable conditions of the poor inhabitants of our town of East Hagbourne'. It is noticeable that almost all the period houses in the village seem to post-date the fire. The Harwell fire is described later. The Upton fire occurred on Whit Tuesday in 1934. It was a very hot day, the men were away in the fields, the women and children on a day's excursion, when the fire broke out at 2 p.m. in the afternoon. By the time it was under control at 4 p.m. the centre of the village had been burnt out. This is why Upton today has so few period houses – they were mostly burnt down.

The nineteenth century saw many events and changes. In the 1830s most of the open fields and commons in these parishes were enclosed, though at Aston Tirrold it occurred in 1743, at Harwell in 1802, and at Blewbury in 1805. Presumably great hardship was caused to the owners of small acreages and to the working class with the loss of the commons. Then the railways were laid down – the Great Western in 1839, and the Didcot, Newbury and Southampton Railway in 1882; with all the disruption caused by the navvies to these peaceful communities, where crime and violence was almost unknown. At the end of the century, Churn Plain became the focus for Army manoeuvres, where summer camps were held every year.

The nineteenth century saw one curious occurrence: this was the discovery of blotting paper at Hagbourne Mill, East Hagbourne. There had been a paper mill at East Hagbourne since the reign of Charles I, and it was owned during that time by the Slade family of Aston Tirrold. It was presumably during the 1830s or 1840s, that a workman forgot to put size into a batch of paper being made. It was thrown aside as waste until John Slade discovered that it was absorbent, and realized its potential. The new product was marketed, and proved very popular, so popular that Hagbourne Mill could not cope with the demand, so the business was transferred to Spalisley Mill in Hampshire. A Mr Ford, husband to John Slade's niece, became the new owner. Mr William Slade won a medal for the finest blotting paper exhibited at the Paris Exhibition of 1855. Hagbourne Mill no longer exists, other than some brick foundations.

Blewbury, at the end of the nineteenth century, was 'discovered' by a different type of newcomer, different that is from the working-class railwaymen of Didcot

New Town; they were artists and writers who found the village to be charming and picturesque, also it was near Didcot station and so they settled there.

It has been during the twentieth century that the villages have had to respond to the greatest changes, especially since the Second World War. There has been a tremendous surge in new house building, both private and public. Also, there has been an 'invasion' of a new kind of villager, one never seen before, whose occupation was not concerned with agriculture – these were the professional middle classes who work outside their villages. Their influx began properly after the First World War, when the working-class agricultural labourers and their families moved out of the old, draughty, damp and primitive period cottages into the new council houses, with hot and cold running water, and other modern conveniences, leaving their former homes to be bought and 'done up' by these newcomers. They had no connection with agriculture, but worked at AERE, Harwell, in local towns or even further afield. Thus agriculture had lost its dominance, but this is not to say that it is not still important – it is, but not as much as in earlier times.

The majority of the illustrations in this book come from postcards, while the remainder are personal photographs. The golden age – if one can call it that – of the postcard lasted for only a brief period, which in this area was roughly from the late 1890s through to the early 1950s. They are no longer produced in such prolific quantities because they are too expensive to publish these days. Though this 'age' may have gone, it did leave behind such a wealth of material, from which many books, such as this one and the rest in this series, are based. The postcard producers, such as Henry Taunt of Oxford, Warland Andrews of Abingdon and Percy Sims of Chipping Norton, were all unknowingly recording for our benefit today, the villages and Didcot, as they appeared over the decades since 1900. This was not their intention; they like any other tradesmen were satisfying a contemporary demand, which was for a constant supply of new and different postcards. They were used for so many purposes, for which we nowadays have specialized cards: they were used as Christmas and birthday cards and in lieu of letters. Today, we would use the telephone. Don Farmborough, an avid collector of postcards, from whose collection the majority of these cards come, estimates that over a thousand postcards were issued covering this area during that 'golden age' of fifty years.

Personal photographs are equally as fascinating, and the older they are the more interesting they become, as many in this book prove. They can reveal so much; different clothes, different styles, but above all they show us a different time, a quieter, more peaceful world, with different backgrounds, to which many people look back with nostalgic longing.

SECTION ONE

Didcot

HOUSES IN WALLINGFORD ROAD, now lower Broadway. Substantially the view is still the same. The Primitive Methodist chapel has gone (now Lay's electrical shop). Barclays Bank occupies the site of the house on the extreme right of the picture, which the bank acquired in 1921, and which has undergone many alterations since. The fourth house down was Didcot's first telegraph exchange.

THE OLD VICARAGE, WALLINGFORD ROAD, built in 1907 by Lady Wantage for her nephew, the Revd Urch. She did not consider that the previous accommodation, a detached house in East Street, was exactly suitable. The photograph dates from around the time of the First World War.

THE OLD POLICE STATION IN HAGBOURNE ROAD, built in 1912. The police occupied the building until 1969, only then transferring to the new station in Mereland Road.

WALLINGFORD ROAD (now lower Broadway) pictured around the time of the First World War.

STATION HILL (as it was known up to the beginning of the Second World War) or Road about 1914. These houses were occupied strictly according to rank within the railway company: the nearer to the station the higher the rank. Thus, the station-master occupied one of the large detached houses near to the station. The small building was Didcot's post office at the time the photograph was taken, during the First World War.

THE CRAFTSMEN AND LABOURERS who were then building the houses in Station Road in 1903, gathered together for their picture to be taken. The Station Road houses were built for their employees by the Great Western Railway Company. To have one's photograph taken then was a novelty. Men of that period always wore hats, as can be seen in this illustration.

LOOKING UP STATION ROAD at the end of the First World War. The land on the other side of the road was then allotments.

HADDON ROAD (now lower Lydalls Road) around about 1914. This was the original name for the whole road which continued through under the railway bridge, to the junction with Abingdon Road. Today, this part of the road is Cow Lane, but it really should be known by the earlier name. Somehow it was changed, colloquially, to Cow Lane, before Didcot's road names were officially established in 1929. The houses and shops in the road were built between 1907 and 1910.

DIDCOT RAILWAY STATION in c. 1920, with hacks awaiting passengers, today's equivalent of the modern taxi.

THE STATION HOTELS in c. 1920. The Prince of Wales and the Great Western Junction Hotel were built 1858–62, and 1846 respectively. The Corn Exchange on market days generated more business when Station Approach (as the area around the station was known then) would be crowded with buyers, farmers, dealers and their workers. The Prince of Wales was actually built in response to the demands of those who attended the Corn Exchange.

STATION MOUND in 1962. It is hard to imagine that this is how the station forecourt appeared in 1962; so tranquil and with so few cars. The mound and its trees have gone in response to the demands made by the motor car. The earth that made up the mound must have been put there when the station was built, having been dug out when the tunnels underneath the station were constructed.

DIDCOT STATION in the early 1970s. Still some years away from the massive alterations of the early 1980s, which have produced the new Didcot Parkway.

THE PROVENDER STORES before the First World War; then a busy, bustling concern as hay, oats and other animal feed-stuff arrived daily by numerous farm wagons. People like Dennis Napper of Manor Farm, and others were contractors who delivered everyday. The animal feed was then transferred to rail wagons and sent all over the region to feed the three thousand or more horses then used by the GWR.

THE INTERIOR OF THE PROVENDER STORES in 1970, a short time before the building was demolished. By then cavernous, empty, deserted, a home for pigeons, it was an eerie place, with rickety cast-iron staircases which threatened to collapse as soon as a foot was placed upon the rungs. It was last used in the early 1950s.

THE FINAL DEMISE OF THE PROVENDER STORES in June 1976. The story from the *Didcot Herald* read: 'Going, going, gone, and down it came in a cloud of dust but it was so massively built that it taxed the strength of the bulldozer and ingenuity of the driver, Mr Lee Bayldon of Huddersfield'.

THE PROVENDER STORES as seen from the meadows, a serene and tranquil scene, on the other side of Foxhall Road some time before the First World War. From March 1915, this field became a muddy site of the future living quarters of the troops building the Arsenal. This is now the site of the Officers' Mess building.

ENTRANCE TO THE CAMP at the end of the First World War, which was then firmly established. It was not long after the outbreak of war that high ranking officers and officials from the War Office were at Didcot inspecting the site. Decisions were quickly made and operations began in March 1915.

THE LIVING QUARTERS, then in huts, at the camp in c. 1917. The huts were in Didcot and the Arsenal/ordnance was on the other side of the railway in Sutton Courtenay. There were so many shells, explosives and other munitions stored that had it all exploded Old Didcot would have disappeared from the map.

ENTRANCE TO THE RAOC CAMP, C. 1929.

ENTRANCE TO THE CAMP, C. 1950.

THE CAMP'S RECREATION HUT, late 1915.

THE INTERIOR OF THE RECREATION HUT, November 1915. For these men, Didcot must have been deadly dull. The young soldier who sent this postcard home to his parents wrote: 'this is where we spend most of our evenings'. There was certainly nowhere else to go, other than the hotels at the station or the Queens Arms. The beer would be more expensive there.

THE YOUNG OFFICER, his NCO and men are from the Arsenal's workshop, Section 32, 1916.

ETON SCHOOLBOYS, including Prince Henry, the future Duke of Gloucester, lined up on Didcot station in November 1915, prior to being marched off to the camp to help unload munitions and supplies. During that November, Colonel Purkiss, officer in charge of the camp, was so overwhelmed by the sheer volume of supplies to be unloaded from railway wagons that he appealed for civilian volunteers to help in the work. Eventually some three thousand volunteers turned up on successive weekends. These Eton schoolboys answered the 'call' of their country.

DIDCOT CORN EXCHANGE photographed just before it was pulled down in the early 1970s. Built in 1857 for local farmers to sell their produce to buyers and dealers from the cities who came down by train on market day. As mentioned previously, it was a busy time for all, the Exchange, the hotels and public houses – the Junction Tap and the old Royal Oak. The Exchange stopped trading sometime between 1906 and 1910. It became a YMCA during the First World War, and continued as such until 1939, when it was converted into the first Station Garage.

THE DIDCOT BRASS BAND outside the YMCA during the early 1920s. This was a very popular band. The Exchange building and its immediate area was known always as the 'Wangle'. This nickname was derived from the red triangle of the sign over the door – it can be seen in the illustration.

DEDICATION OF THE WAR MEMORIAL to those who fell in the First World War. It was sited in the grounds of St Peter's church, Northbourne. The ceremony took place on 15 May 1921.

GERMAN PRISONERS OF WAR, 1947. After the war and before repatriation, these prisoners of war were moved to Didcot, where they occupied tented quarters, sited on what is now Newlands Avenue. They were well known in the area, and became friendly with Didcot residents. Hans Plahta, who was a fighter pilot, stayed on after the war, and moved to Cheltenham where he now lives – he is the man outside the tent. The other two men are unknown.

THE ATS CAMP, UPPER STATION ROAD, October 1969. This is now the site of the local council's housing estate of Great Western Drive. During the Second World War, there was a very large work force, both service and civilian, working at the camp. This camp was one of many that was erected to house this work force. There was one on Ryman's Meadow (now Blenheim Drive) and one on what would be the future Newlands Avenue housing estate – this is where the German prisoners of war were held.

A VE DAY PARTY in Tavistock Avenue, May 1945.

THE OLD NORTHBOURNE CHURCH OF ENGLAND SCHOOL in 1967, which was demolished in the early 1970s. Erected in 1877, enlarged in 1892 and 1894 to take 250 pupils; its first headmaster was the formidable Mr G.R. MacFarlane. The old building was too small, so it was replaced in the early 1960s by the modern school in Cockcroft Avenue.

CHILDREN FROM NORTHBOURNE SCHOOL in the early 1900s. Mr MacFarlane stands on the extreme left, no doubt keeping an eye on the children. Woe betide any child that should move, let alone speak.

CHILDREN IN THE EARLY 1950s at play at the old Northbourne school.

TWO SCENES FROM DIDCOT CARNIVALS of the early 1930s. These were tremendous affairs, very popular, not only with Didcot people but with the villages as well, who would enter floats. The Harwell fire brigade was very enthusiastic. Their 1930 float is pictured below in Foxhall Road. The other photograph of horse and carriage was taken in lower Broadway.

THE OLD FIRE STATION in Wessex Road became operational on 17 July 1929. The brigade was at first a local affair, the building provided by the Wallingford Rural District Council who also paid for all the equipment. But the firemen were all volunteers. It was during the Second World War, that the brigade was taken over by the national force. The new station in the Broadway was opened in 1953, making the old building redundant. Today it houses the local office of the South Oxfordshire District Council.

DIDCOT'S FIRST FIRE ENGINE, which was pulled by horses. It is worlds away from the modern fire engines of today. Fires of yesterday, like the Upton fire of 1934, could not now happen with today's modern appliances. The fire engines would be there and the fire out before even one house was consumed.

ONE OF DIDCOT'S FIRST FIRE CREWS, all volunteers. They are sitting on and arranged around the fire engine of 1929, as pictured on the previous page. Mr James Morse is the civilian in the top row and Sergeant Perry is in the second row, his hands resting on the man in front. Taken in the Broadway, outside what is now Barclays Bank.

THE YOUNG MR LEN HITCHCOCK of Kynaston Road some time in the early 1930s, in Park Road. He was then employed as a milkboy by S.H. Pengilley of the Parade, lower Broadway. The Parade is the long terrace of shops on the lower Broadway, which Mr Pengilley built in 1930, see illustration on p. 50.

WESSEX AND KYNASTON ROADS in c. 1931. These two roads were built as part of the Wallingford Rural District Council housing estate, erected between 1920 and 1934. The estate was built in response to the housing famine caused by the siting of the Royal Army Ordnance Corp's Arsenal at Didcot from 1915 onwards. The Arsenal or the Depot, as it was more commonly known, grew steadily in size during the 1920s and 1930s. It could be argued that all the development of those years came as a direct result of the Army coming to Didcot.

SPIRAL DEVELOPMENT OF WANTAGE ROAD (now upper Broadway) and Park Road continued apace during the 1920s. This postcard dates from around 1929.

GLYN AVENUE WAS CONSTRUCTED in 1927. At the end of the next year, the contractors, unable to find buyers for their new houses, offered the street of houses and eight in Vauxhall Lane to the local council – an offer which was accepted. This is why these houses are council-owned and the rest of the estate, then called the Georgetown Garden City Estate, is in private hands. The council paid £375 for three-bedroom houses, and £325 for those with two bedrooms.

HOUSES IN PARK ROAD, in the early 1930s. The houses on the right were built by a Mr Colbourne of the Swindon Construction Company in 1934, after whom Colbourne Road is named.

HOUSES IN FOXHALL ROAD, built in 1933 by Blake Bros.

SHOPS IN WANTAGE ROAD, 1935. The detached house on the extreme right was the home of Major Nott of the Didcot Building Company, which built these shops. His company also erected a row of terraced houses lower down Park Road, opposite the Royal Oak.

SHERWOOD ROAD in 1934.

DIDCOT'S FIRST CINEMA which opened in 1927 was erected by Mr W.E. Cullen. The board advertises an early programme, of *Tom Mix, The Lost World* and *The Gay Cavalier*. The cinema was a runaway success, attracting customers from Didcot and the villages around, so much so that a new one was built later in 1935 – the present building. The old cinema just could not cope with the demand.

NEW HOUSE AND OUTBUILDINGS at the corner of Foxhall Road, owned by Mr Bowering, who converted the latter into a garage in 1931. This building was demolished in the early 1960s, to make way for a new garage.

WHEN A TOWN'S POPULATION INCREASES, it is not long before the necessary services, such as churches, schools and shops, follow along with public houses and clubs, which could be said by some to be equally important. The Marlborough Club in the Broadway was opened by the Duke of Marlborough in December 1927. The Wallingford Arms was built the next year. The two postcards date from c. 1931.

THIS WAS THE VIEW that could be seen from the top of the new Coronet Cinema in summer 1940, looking north-east to the station. The farmland was Ryman's Meadow and the houses are those in Garth Road and Melton Drive. The photographer was Mr Thomas Dines of King Alfred Drive, who was the cinema's projectionist. Hard to believe that this was at that time the centre of Didcot.

LOOKING DOWN THE WANTAGE ROAD in c. 1920. Today, Haydon Road would be on the left of the picture.

LOOKING UP THE HARWELL ROAD in 1928. Before Didcot's roads were properly named in 1929, these two postcards provide a good example of the confusion that then existed over road names: though they stood only about 20 yards away when taking the photographs, to one it was the Wantage Road, to the other Harwell Road. After 1929, all confusion ended, by naming the road Broadway.

A LATER POSTCARD OF THE BROADWAY of 1934; taken at the time the Haydon Road houses were being built. The notice read: 'Freehold plots for sale'. Also it seems that Haydon Road itself had not long been laid down.

THE BROADWAY in c. 1931. W.H. Smith had just completed the building of their shop (on the right) having moved up to the Broadway from their tin hut opposite Cow Lane railway bridge, a site then known as the 'Quadrant'. W.H. Smith stayed in this shop until the early 1970s, when they moved to their present position.

MR W.J. STREET in the doorway of his shop, greeting customers, some time after the war. This shop, now an optician's, is next to the dry cleaners adjacent to the market. The notice in his window reads: 'Ideal Xmas presents. Fancy boxes of chocolates at PRE-WAR prices by leading manufacturers. Inspect our interior display'. Mr Street was better known as a photographer; many of his framed photographs still hang on living-room walls throughout the district.

THE NEW WHITE HART just after being built.

Left:

THE OLD WHITE HART had become too small by 1927 for the demands put upon it by more and more customers, whose numbers had increased as the town grew. It had been built in 1847 to cater for trade that had been created by the siting of the railway station at Didcot. The construction of Station Road in 1844/5 had meant an increasing volume of traffic using this and the Wallingford Road, but by the mid-1920s, the pub had to be replaced, and so it was by the new White Hart. The photograph shows the point in time when the two pubs – the old and the new – existed side by side. The present pub has been renamed the Broadway.

S.20017. THE PARADE, DIDCOT.

THE PARADE IN LOWER BROADWAY. All these shops, including the bank building and Pengilley's Parade, were built between 1928 and 1930.

JOBS DAIRY in the lower Broadway, built in 1935. Later it became the Express Dairy, who closed their business, and sold the site to a developer. A housing estate now occupies its former grounds.

ST FRIEDWIDE'S CHURCH in 1967. Formerly an old barn built after enclosure in the 1840s, and with the growth of the various estates centred around Park Road, it became redundant. There was an urgent need for a church here, and the building was acquired by the Church authorities in 1935 and converted into a mission hall. Later in October 1940, it was further consecrated as the mission church of St Friedwide's. Back in the nineteenth century, a young man, jilted by his girlfriend, hanged himself, either in or outside the barn. For years afterwards, villagers would not pass the barn at night for fear of seeing his ghost. During the early 1970s, the church was burnt down by an arsonist.

SINCE THE FIRST WORLD WAR, every decade saw changes which had not generally been recorded. This situation was remedied in the 1970s by the compiler who took these photographs of buildings or views that have now been either demolished or covered by new housing estates. The building above formerly housed the Rural District Council offices which were sited opposite the Post Office. It was formerly the old St Peters vicarage, which was sold to the RDC in the early 1950s. It was extended by the Churchill Annexe. It, too, became redundant when the new local authority built its headquarters at Crowmarsh, and the old building was demolished. The new Baptist House now occupies its former site.

THE TREES AND THE PATH over the old railway formerly led to the original Fleet Meadow. It is now a housing estate.

THIS TRANQUIL FIELD with grazing cows formerly at the back of Norreys Road, now the Barleyfields-Wheatfields housing estate – but it was never that . . .

JUNCTION TAP, then derelict, was demolished in 1988. Built in 1846 as a pub and part of the Great Western Junction Hotel, there was a strict class demarcation: the hotel was for farmers and other middle-class travellers, while the Tap was for the working class. These lines have now merged so the Tap was another Didcot building that became redundant.

THE HAGBOURNE ROAD RAILWAY BRIDGE. With the closure of the Didcot, Newbury and Southampton Railway line in c. 1964, the bridge became increasingly unsafe so that finally it had to be demolished. It was built at a time when traffic consisted of the odd horse and cart, not heavy lorries. This happened in the mid-1970s.

THE RAILWAY BRIDGE over lower Broadway in the early 1960s. It too was demolished when the Fleetway housing estate was being built.

SECTION TWO

Blewbury and Upton

BLEWBURTON HILL at the turn of the twentieth century. Although it is partly in the parish of Aston Tirrold, it is associated more with Blewbury. The hill is a former Iron-Age fort of pre-Roman Conquest date. A Bronze-Age village of the fourth century BC was first sited there, defended by a palisade. This was followed by Iron-Age fortifications of c. 300 BC. These fortifications were renewed during the second century BC. Archaelogical evidence suggests that the fort was successfully attacked either by the Belgae or the Romans. There was some settlement here during Romano-British times.

BLEWBURY IN THE DISTANCE, at the turn of the twentieth century, seen from the south-west and from the Chalk Pits.

Entrance to Village. Blewbury

TWO VIEWS OF THE OLD BARLEY MOW, dating from around the First World War, and looking both up and down London Road – then a very quiet village street. The pub was burnt down in 1924. It was then the first building to be encountered on entering the village from Streatley and the east. The first mention of the house as a public house is in 1814. To the right was a spot to the south of the road called Hunts Grave. 'Grave' is thought to be a corruption of 'Grove'; but there was once in circulation a story that Hunt was the last highwayman to be hanged in these parts, and it was the site of his grave.

LOOKING WEST ALONG LONDON ROAD. The house on the immediate left, now Meers Parcel, was formerly a pub, the Catherine Wheel, until 1926. Its old name was Shernes and it seems to have been converted into a pub sometime at the end of the eighteenth century. The barns opposite were converted into housing units during the mid-1950s.

LOOKING EAST ALONG LONDON ROAD, sometime during the late 1940s.

MISS RICHARDSON with some of her pupils c. 1885. She ran a 'day and boarding school' at Treble House Terrace, London Road, from around 1865 to 1890, to which most of the farmers and tradesmen's children went. These small private schools were to be found in every village, including Didcot, before the Second World War, but since then they have just disappeared. The group are, top row, left to right: Florrie Robinson, Ernest Hall, Selwyn Caudwell, Ada Hall, Agnes Abbott, Roland Caudwell and Rosa Robinson. Middle row: Daisy Richardson, Miss Richardson and Winnie Richardson. Bottom row: Frank Robinson, Hilda Caudwell, Blanche Robinson and Emily Lousley. In that one photograph are represented all the prominent farming families of Blewbury during the nineteenth century, the Robinsons, Lousleys and Caudwells.

THE GABLES, as the house was known up to 1954, now named Turnpike House. The gate on the turnpike road from Harwell to Streatley was located outside the house, hence the name.

FRED STREET (wearing the rosette) and Edwin Greenough at the time of the First World War celebrations of 1919, standing beside their wagon in the yard of the Gables.

THE CHURN PLAIN became annually the venue for military summer camps, where volunteers were trained, from the 1890s onwards. Here, on the Pound, the Band of the Royal Irish Fusiliers entertain villagers in September 1905.

THE WESTERN END OF LONDON ROAD, c. 1949. The inn sign hanging on the left is for the New Inn, formerly the King William, and now the Bluebury Inn. The houses beyond are Felixstowe Cottage, and the timbered house, Double Doors, which is said to be the oldest house in Blewbury.

ENTRANCE TO THE VILLAGE, from the western end. On the right Double Doors and to the left the farm buildings of Ashbrook Farm.

NOTTINGHAM FEE, early 1920s. The house is Hall Barn Close, Chapel Lane, with the Red Lion beyond. William Rushton, the artist, had his studio here.

THREE SIMILAR VIEWS OF WESTBROOK STREET, but taken over a very long period, and showing little change. The last is a Taunt card, taken around 1905, while the other two date to the beginning of the First World War, and to the late 1940s. The row of houses are Brookside (the timbered house), Wayside Cottage and Martins. The last was formerly a Particular Baptist chapel, built by Francis Martin in 1843. It had ceased to be a chapel by 1870. Miss Martin had a fancy goods shop here earlier this century. Finally, at the far end is the forge.

THE OLD RED LION, CHAPEL LANE, early 1930s. One of Blewbury's oldest pubs, but there is no evidence to say when this eighteenth-century house was thus converted.

CHILDREN GATHERED TOGETHER to give depth and interest to this early photograph of the house, Stocks, Hall Barn Close and the Red Lion in the early 1900s. Stocks had been converted into two cottages sometime in the eighteenth or nineteenth century; one way of creating more housing. It continued as two cottages until 1930. Hall Barn Close must date to the sixteenth century.

BLEWBURY'S FAMOUS COB WALLS at the beginning of the First World War; the path is a continuation of Red Lion Lane.

LAURENCES (centre) with Nottingham Fee Cottage in the background, sometime between the wars. The nearest house is Nottingham Fee Studio. Laurences is the only property in Blewbury to retain its original name from the survey of 1548.

CHURCH ROAD. The tower of St Michael's in the distance, the gable end of the Malthus school house showing through the trees and the house Swallows at the end of the road. This picture is post-war.

THE PARISH CHURCH OF ST MICHAEL'S, c. 1905. Originally a twelfth-century (c. 1190) cruciform building with a central tower, to which a north aisle was added in the fourteenth, and a south aisle and western tower in the fifteenth century. The central tower was then demolished.

THE VICARAGE WAS BUILT in 1872 at a cost of nearly £2,000 – an enormous sum for those days, especially when one considers that the average farm labourer was getting just 10 s. (50p) a week. It was built for the coming of a new vicar, the Revd John Burgess (1870–90); a barrister turned parson, he and his wife were full of 'good works' around the village. From 1904 to 1913, the vicar was the Revd Victor Lorenzo Whitechurch, a prolific and successful novelist. Two books *Downland Corner* and *Downland Echoes* are solidly based on the village. From 1963 until his recent retirement, the vicar was the Revd Hugh Pickles who was a well-loved man and an ardent cricketer, for which he will always be remembered. He died not long ago.

CLEVE COTTAGE, CHAPEL LANE, c. 1912. Part of the house during the late nineteenth century was possibly a shop – one of the parlour shops so common – then a grocery shop, afterwards a milliners and finally a sweet shop, run by Mrs Bowen.

LANTERN COTTAGE in South Street, in the late 1940s. It was a blacksmith's shop in the 1840s, then occupied by Job Huggill, a watchmaker. Lately, it has been a very popular tea-shop.

ABNERS, formerly known as Pigeons. The 'new' name comes from two of its former nineteenth-century owners – the Abner Graces, both of whom were parish clerks at the end of that century. It has its own history like any other old house. Inside carved on a beam is 'I.A.L 1651' these are probably the initials of a member of the Lewendon family. It has been a Methodist chapel and a private school.

THE SHOP OF JOHN BILLSON (standing in the door) in Church Road. The shop has gone, a victim of the times; it closed in 1976, and is now a private house. Abners can be seen at the other end of the terrace.

OUTSIDE THE LOAD OF MISCHIEF, probably Blewbury's oldest pub, in South Street. George Green (he stands hatless), the licensee, and some of his customers, possibly in the 1890s. The most intriguing thing about the pub is its sign, which could be said to be quite infamous, as it is copied from an original painted by Hogarth for a London inn in the early eighteenth century. There is another copy at Cambridge, and a similar sign shows a man chained to his wife. There is a rhyme that should by rights go with the sign: 'A Monkey, a magpie and a wife, is the true emblem of strife'.

South Street, Blewbury

SOUTH STREET in the late 1920s. On the left is the Load of Mischief with Rose Cottage on the right. The earlier name for the latter was Slades, a family name.

CHURCH END WITH BROOK COTTAGE and Carpenters, early 1920s.

LOOKING SOUTH DOWN SOUTH STREET EARLY 1920s. Holt Cottage is on the left.

LOOKING UP SOUTH STREET. Sawyers Arms and Holly Tree Cottage, with Holt Cottage in the distance. The Sawyers Arms was the shortest lived of all Blewbury's pubs. Its name came from a saw pit that was in a nearby garden. It was in the garden to the pub that T.F.M. Sheard painted the *Gossipping Gaffers*, one of which was Robert Herridge, a well-known rustic poet. The painting now hangs in the Central Library at Oxford. The pub was demolished in 1964.

OUTSIDE THE SAWYERS ARMS, possibly in 1897; the flag may be for Queen Victoria's Diamond Jubilee celebrations in that year. Abraham Street, the licensee, is holding the hand of his daughter, Mabel. His wife, Louisa, stands in the doorway. Mabel Street, then Westbury, kept the pub until 1964.

DRAGONWYCK AND WINDING WAY, both seventeenth-century houses, in South Street, around the time of the First World War. Dragonwyck was known as Slades in the eighteenth century. Both houses were owned for a long period by the Lousleys during the nineteenth century.

BERRY LANE in the 1920s.

DIBLEYS, an early seventeenth-century house, off South Street, in 1916. It seems to have acquired its name from a John Dibley who bought the property in 1738. He sold the property to Thomas Humfrey in 1797. The property was known as Dods alias Coxs before Dibley's time. Dibley's housing estate was built in 1969.

ANOTHER VIEW OF DIBLEYS, seen from the other side, late 1920s.

THE BLEWBURY ALMSHOUSES, near to the churchyard of St Michael's in c. 1910.

THE OLD MILL, off Berry Lane and north of Manor Farm, was probably sited on that of one of the original Domesday mills. It was always leased with the manor until the breaking up and the sale away from the Lockinge Estate after the death of Lady Wantage in 1921. This vast estate, consisting of some 20,000 acres in North Berkshire, had to be broken up to pay death duties. The mill cottage attached to the mill was built in 1824 by Joseph Lousley, who was tenant of the manor. The mill ceased active milling around 1930. This view is c. 1905.

ANOTHER VIEW OF THE MILL, this time much later, possibly in the early 1930s.

THE BLEWBURY POSTMAN, commonly known as Mr Y or Mr Who, around the turn of the century.

CARPENTERS COTTAGE, South Street, early 1920s. An early seventeenth-century house, which was, in 1800, the dwelling house for a busy farm. Now all that remains is the house. It was once occupied by a George Knapp, who died in 1818, and left this salutary warning to his family, in the south porch of the church – 'Dear wife and children as you pass by, as you are now, once was I. As I am now so must you be, Therefore be prepared to follow me.' It must have embarrassed them every time they passed by into the church.

LIKE MANY HOUSES IN THE AREA, and with the steady engrossment of farms during the eighteenth and nineteenth centuries, Sheencroft lost its status as the centre of a farm and was reduced to and divided up into three cottages for farm workers. It has now reverted back to a home for one family.

THE DOWNS AT CHURN were used by the Army from 1889 onwards to train volunteers from territorial and reserve units; and summer camps, from early May to mid-September, were held every year until the First World War. The Army's use of the Churn Plain, a vast, flat area ideal for military manoeuvres, was made possible by the presence of the Didcot, Newbury and Southampton Railway and its small halt at Churn. The halt had been hastily erected in June 1888, just in time for the National Rifle Association's annual competition to be held the following month. But the association rejected Churn in favour of Bisley, which was nearer to London, as the former was very isolated. The prime mover in the projected transfer was Lord Wantage, who was both a prominent member of the association and a director of the railway company. The Downs were so isolated that the railway was the only means of access for supplies and a link to the outside world. During those two decades, every summer would see up to two thousand men encamped at Churn. The effect that these men had on Blewbury, small and isolated before their coming, as they descended on the village daily, can be imagined. Each day horses were brought to the village for watering and water carts trundled to and fro all day. The village shops catered for large number of troops who became new customers. Everyone, farmers, tradespeople, benefited from their presence. Water was a continual problem. The above illustration shows Corporal King and men of the Royal Engineers at Ashbrook Farm, London Road, pumping water up to Churn, on 29 September 1894.

THE PUMPING STATION AT ASHBROOK FARM, 29 September 1894.

THE CAMP of 200 Royal Field Artillery in command of Major Battiscombe, Bridus Meadow, Blewbury, August 1907.

THE CAMP AT BLEWBURY, 1890; the 8th and 14th Hussars, looking east, Blewbury on the left.

THE CHURN CAMP, September 1905.

ELI CAUDWELL OF ASHBROOK FARM, with his steam plough in 1892. He was a forward-looking man, quite receptive to new ideas and new methods. The steam plough was a good example of his modern innovations.

PLOUGHING AT BLEWBURY in the nineteenth century and haymaking at East Hagbourne between the wars.

HIGH STREET, UPTON, in the early years of the twentieth century. The cottages, outside of which the man is standing, have now been pulled down.

TWO COTTAGES IN STREAM ROAD, Upton, sometime in the 1930s. This was known then in the village as Frog Alley.

THE GEORGE AND DRAGON AT UPTON, C. 1908; then run by George Summersby. Mrs Summersby is the woman in the middle, and the child in front of her is Doris, her daughter. Aunt Alice is the lady with the walking stick. The other woman is unknown. The 'little girl' died in 1988, aged eighty-six. The main part of the house is probably seventeenth century, and was extended in the Victorian period.

THE LAST TRAIN THROUGH UPTON STATION, 8 September 1962. The Didcot, Newbury and Southampton Railway, the northern stretch of which opened in April 1882. It ran from Didcot to Upton and Blewbury, Compton, Hermitage, Newbury and thence to Southampton. It never really made money, even when the train was the only means of long-distance transport. Throughout most of its history, it was a single track line; only since the last war were there two tracks – this was done by the Americans to increase its capacity to carry war supplies. Finally, in 1962, under the Beeching Plan, the line was closed.

East Hagbourne

THE FORD AT EAST HAGBOURNE, C. 1910, and in the background the Spread Eagle; a scene that is now greatly changed. The ford was a perennial problem to the local authority. Each year a tremendous flood would make the road completely impassable. Presumably in the age of the horse and cart it did not matter so much, but the motor car demanded drier conditions than this, so eventually the ford was bridged in the early 1920s. The Spread Eagle is East Hagbourne's newest pub, becoming one sometime in the 1900s. In 1900, the house was called Willow Place, and was a private house. Presumably, the pub was established to cater for customers living on the southern edge of the village and from Blewbury way. It does seem that for most of its history, it was a beer house. Only in 1953 did it receive a spirit licence.

HOUSES IN FIELDSIDE, 1920s.

ANOTHER VIEW OF FIELDSIDE, late 1920s.

LOOKING UP BLEWBURY ROAD towards the Lower Cross, C. 1910. The wall of Lower End Farm is to the right, and on the left, the nearest house is Cobblestones, from the late seventeenth century. The timbered house at the end of this group of houses has been demolished. Bungalows now occupy its former site.

LOOKING UP BLEWBURY ROAD, somewhat earlier in c. 1905, showing Whites the butcher's shop, the Primitive chapel of 1884, and Whitechapel Cottages to the left.

LOOKING DOWN THE BLEWBURY ROAD in the early 1930s. There is hardly any change: the motor car has yet to make its impact on the environment.

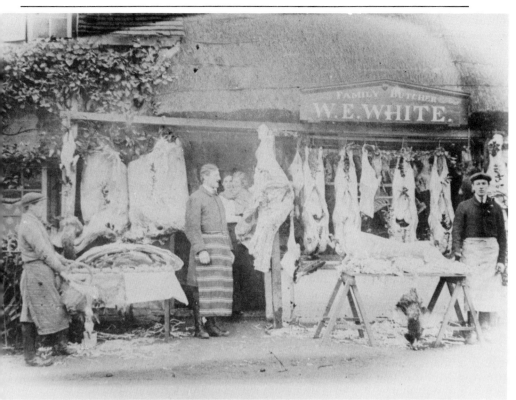

WHITES THE BUTCHERS, c. 1912. The group in front of the shop are, from left to right: Will Eustace, William White, Mrs White, her daughter, Hilda, and Will Painter at the far right. At that time they only sold local meat which was slaughtered at the back of the shop. This family butchers has been trading here on the same premises, for over a hundred years and is, unusually, still trading, run by Mr William White's nephew. So many other village butchers have closed over the past twenty years. In the 1960s, there were three at Harwell, and all are now closed. Competition from the big supermarkets is too great.

THE TRAVELLERS WELCOME at the end of the nineteenth century; a postcard by Warland Andrews of Abingdon. His cards are so distinctive. He must have spent some time before he took the photograph in gathering children together to give interest; he was much more of an artist than any of his competitors, such as Taunt. The pub may be late eighteenth century in date, for it seems to be represented on the map of East Hagbourne of 1775. Village pubs before the First World War tended to act as working men's clubs, where the village men would congregate at night after their day's hard labour, and over their single half pint (for this would be all they could afford; even with beer at 2 d. a pint), talk and sing traditional songs, many sad and mournful. If anyone wishes to get a true picture of the pub at this time, they should read chapter four of Flora Thompson's *Larkrise to Candleford*. At the Travellers Welcome in 1865 the publican was Benjamin Bosley.

GRANGE COTTAGE, a mid-seventeenth-century house, with an early eighteenth-century frontage, at Lower Cross sometime at the end of the nineteenth century.

GRANGE COTTAGE AND LOWER CROSS, at the beginning of the First World War. Lower down Blewbury Road can be seen the timbered house of seventeenth-century date, which has now been demolished.

Lower Cross, East Hagbourne

LOWER CROSS AND LOWER CROSS COTTAGE, possibly in the 1920s. The Cross has now been converted into the First World War Memorial.

EAST HAGBOURNE 19

LOWER CROSS COTTAGES during the early 1930s. This is a house, converted into two cottages, of mid-seventeenth-century date.

LOOKING UP MAIN ROAD towards Lower Cross, early 1930s. Green Shutters is the house nearest the camera, with Buckles farther down the road. Both houses are mid-seventeenth century in date.

THE GABLES AND GREEN SHUTTERS, looking up Main Road, in the late 1940s.

ANOTHER VIEW, but looking down the road, early 1930s.

THE GABLES, c. 1931. A mid-seventeenth-century house with three gabled dormer windows.

HIGHER UP MAIN ROAD, late 1940s. On the left, Apple Tree Cottage, the pub, Fleur de Lys, the old Greyhound pub, now Sundial Cottage, and at the far end, the post office. Interestingly, all the cottages (except the post office which probably dates to the 1870s), are dated by the Department of Environment to the mid-seventeenth century: were they all built after the Great Fire of 1659? It does seem that every house in the village except the church was burnt down. There is only one house in the village which is dated to the sixteenth century and that is Kingsholm, on the south side of Main Road.

THE POST OFFICE AND SHOP in Main Road, c. 1910, with, possibly, Mr Albert Mobbs at the doorway of his shop. This building was probably erected in the 1870s (it appears on the 25 inch OS map of c. 1880) by Edward Wakefield, the village grocer and baker. Before he moved to the new shop, his earlier premises had been in Church Close Cottages (see p. 112). Mr Wakefield was a prominent Methodist, and an elder of the chapel in the Wallingford Road, Didcot, which has now been demolished. He was certainly involved in the purchase of land and the building of the chapel in 1868, and it was the first building to be erected in Northbourne. He probably also had a similar function with the erection of the chapel in Blewbury Road in 1884. The post office and shop were sold by 1900 to Mr Albert Mobbs, who will no doubt be remembered by many of the older villagers. He continued to trade there until the 1930s, when the business was sold to Mr Douglas Heard, who was trading there in 1939. Mr Heard continued in business until the early 1950s. The post office passed through more hands, and today it no longer functions as a shop but is now an art gallery, run by Mrs Jennie Kuca.

ANOTHER VIEW OF THE POST OFFICE, C. 1914.

MR DOUGLAS HEARD AND FAMILY, 1940s.

LOOKING UP MAIN ROAD, C. 1900. The Greyhound pub has gone, having closed down during the early 1920s, but it was still there at the beginning of the First World War. The Greyhound, in company with all other pubs in East Hagbourne (excepting the Spread Eagle), was trading before 1860; but the histories of these pubs are not known. It is strange to think that during those years before the First World War, five pubs were open, and making a profit, whereas today with a larger and richer population, only three pubs remain. Is this because of insufficient trade or higher financial demands made on the publican and brewery company? In the 1860s, the only tax that a publican would be liable to pay was the poor rate.

LOOKING DOWN MAIN ROAD, past the Fleur de Lys, a seventeenth-century house, now a pub, at the beginning of the First World War. The Greyhound is still trading for its sign is still there. Bay Cottage, an eighteenth-century building, is on the right.

ANOTHER VIEW OF THE ROAD and the Fleur de Lys, but much later, in the early 1930s. Two buildings have gone: the barn between Fleur de Lys and the Greyhound (now Sundial Cottage) and a house that was next door to Bay Cottage.

A FOOTPATH AT THE BACK of East Hagbourne, early 1930s.

PARSONAGE FARM on the south side of Main Road, c. 1931. A very fine house of two differing architectural dates: the earliest part is seventeenth century, but incorporating even earlier work plus an early eighteenth-century casing, possibly of Queen Anne date.

UPPER CROSS AND MAIN ROAD, C. 1910. The three crosses are dated to the fifteenth century by the Department of the Environment, but they are possibly earlier than this: a survey of the Manor of West Hagbourne of 1411, writes about a 'messuage [a house] at the High Cross in the vill of Westhakebourne'. This 'High Cross' must be that at Coscote. Such crosses are thought to be sanctuary crosses, marking the area of retreat for medieval refugees; and were badly damaged during the Civil War, as outward symbols for papists. The Crosses in East Hagbourne have been restored: Upper Cross during the nineteenth century, and Lower Cross as the village's war memorial.

ANOTHER VIEW, C. 1905.

CHURCH CLOSE, looking towards the Cross, early 1930s.

East Hagbourne Cross & Village.

THIS VIEW – or one of the many variations – of East Hagbourne has been photographed so many times. This one dates to the early years of the First World War. East Hagbourne at the Upper Cross has always been considered – and rightly so – as one of the most picturesque views in the area. Postcard publishers have always regarded it so, ever since the days of Warland Andrews and Henry Taunt.

UPPER CROSS AND CHURCH CLOSE COTTAGES, **early** 1930s.

THE CROSS, church and Upper Cross Cottages, c. 1900. It is the juxtaposition of these three elements: cross, church and cottages which makes this part of East Hagbourne so very picturesque.

UPPER CROSS COTTAGES, c. 1914. A terrace of three cottages of mid-seventeenth-century date; the large timber framing has been infilled with red brick in a herringbone pattern. It is part jettied and there is a cross-wing to the right.

THE CHURCH OF ST MICHAEL. The earliest part of the church is dated to the twelfth century, and this is the nave. There is an arcade of 1190, and an even earlier chancel arch of 1150. The north aisle and vestry were built in 1350, along with the north doorway. Later between 1450 and 1500 the decorated east window was added, so too was the battlemented tower. The village is famous for its campanological skills, and a familiar sound on still summer evenings is the peal of bells. There are eight bells, the earliest dates to 1602. The pinnacled octagonal bellcot is high on the east side and contains the original fleur de lys decorated bell, for the installation of which Alice Aldworth, of West Hagbourne, paid 16 pence in 1545. Inside the church there are some interesting brasses: Hugh and Christian Keeles of 1613 and 1627; Clarice de Windsor, lady of West Hagbourne Manor of 1403; John York of 1413; and John York and wife of 1445. Recently discovered on the wall of the north aisle are the Royal Arms of Charles II, and the Hanoverian Arms.

THE CROSS, CHURCH and Edward Wakefield's first shop at No. 1 Upper Cross Cottages. The photograph is said to date to 1871, when Wakefield was still trading here and before the post office shop was built. Interestingly, cottages are shown in Church Path, behind the Cross. These had been demolished by the time the first edition, 25 inch, OS map had been issued; they are not shown on the map of 1880.

LOOKING UP MAIN ROAD, towards the Croft and Tudor House, early 1930s.

LOOKING DOWN TOWARDS THE CROSS. Tudor House on the left, and in the distance, behind the Cross, is Fletchers, another mid-seventeenth-century house.

TUDOR HOUSE, photographed sometime in the late 1930s. Once again, a late seventeenth-century house; large timber framing, and part-jettied. One interesting feature is the great central brick chimney stack of diagonally set flues. There is a single-storeyed wing, attached to which is a thatched barn.

TWO VIEWS OF EAST HAGBOURNE SCHOOL, one of which looks down towards the Cross and Fletchers. The school was built in 1874 by the National Society, for 190 children, and was enlarged in 1965. There had been a school earlier in 1847, controlled by the church and vestry, who appointed the school teachers. Billings Directory of 1865 states that there are schools for boys and girls.

CHILDREN AT HAGBOURNE SCHOOL, with Mr Parsons, the headmaster, in 1957.

CHILDREN AT HAGBOURNE SCHOOL, 1951.

THE BOOT PUBLIC HOUSE as seen from the east meadow in the late 1940s. The house, possibly seventeenth century, was certainly there in 1775; it is shown on the map of that year. It was a pub in the mid-1860s, when Joseph Napper was the licensee; Charles Napper followed him as publican in 1891. In those days the Nappers were running all Hagbourne's pubs, including the Horse and Harrow at West Hagbourne. In the mid-1860s, Ambrose Napper (he built the cottages at Marsh Bridge, Didcot) was at the Greyhound; William Napper, the Fleur de Lys, (he was also the village blacksmith); and Joseph Napper, at the Horse and Harrow, West Hagbourne. Ben Bosley ran the Travellers Welcome. The Boot is now a private house; like many other pubs in the district it became no longer financially viable. Thomas Cox was the last in a long line of licensees, he closed the pub in 1959.

COSCOT MANOR in c. 1929. The house is now divided in two, one part is still known as Coscot Manor, the other is Yew Tree Farm. Originally there was no Coscot Manor, only the manors of East and West Hagbourne. Coscot in the medieval period was a small hamlet, which over the centuries had been reduced to two or three cottages. In 1555, there seem to have been around ten cottages. The house, Coscot Manor, was very probably built by Thomas Sawyer, a member of the Sawyer family of East Hagbourne and Didcot. In 1628, he sold a house and 48 acres of land to Richard Sawyer of Didcot; and that house could only have been Coscot Manor.

West Hagbourne

DOWN FARM, OF WEST HAGBOURNE, C. 1929. Down Farm is now situated on the western outskirts of Didcot, but still in West Hagbourne. Much of its former farmland is now covered by Didcot housing, such as Norreys Road, Barleyfields and Wheatfields, and even Didcot's public park was formerly. The farmhouse is another seventeenth-century house and was built after a partial enclosure of West Hagbourne's common land – Hagbourne Down. These commons were known as the Sheep and Cow commons.

LOOKING UP YORK ROAD, West Hagbourne, at the turn of the twentieth century. Woodleys is on the right, dated 1688, and York Farm Cottages on the left. All are seventeenth century in date.

ANOTHER VIEW OF YORK ROAD, in the late 1930s. Woodleys is one of the few houses in the villages in this area still to be named after a family. The Woodleys were at West Hagbourne and Didcot in the early eighteenth century, and are still living in these two places.

Old Cottages, West Hagbourne

LOOKING DOWN YORK ROAD towards Main Street, sometime between the wars, York Farm Cottages on the left. The two cottages in Main Street were demolished before the Second World War. They were seventeenth-century in date.

WEST HAGBOURNE H

ANOTHER VIEW OF YORK ROAD, down to Main Street, in the early 1930s.

MAIN STREET PRE-WAR, showing Thatched Cottage and Wycherts, both of seventeenth-century date.

MAIN STREET, looking up towards York Road with Wycherts to the left. Early 1930s.

MAIN STREET, with Ivy Farm, an eighteenth-century house, taken in the early 1930s.

BLISSETTS (seventeenth century) opposite the village pond, in the early 1930s.

THE HORSE AND HARROW, under snow, sometime in the 1920s. The house is possibly early eighteenth century in date. It was there in 1759 trading as an inn. It is quite clearly shown on the map of West Hagbourne of 1759, which is primitively drawn and an inn sign is crudely sketched in. At that time this corner was known as Stotland Ash, and it was still known as such in recent times. This local place name comes from the Stotland family that had land here; Thomas Stotland held a tenement from the manor of West Hagbourne in 1368.

Harwell

AN AERIAL VIEW OF HARWELL in 1944. Looking west from the church.

KINGSWALL RESTAURANT, in the early 1970s. The line of the new road (the A34) can just be seen in front of the restaurant, in the immediate foreground. The premises have been much enlarged since this photograph was taken. In the early 1950s, it was still two small cottages.

THIS POSTCARD IS ENTITLED THE READING ROAD, but it is really the Hollow Way, the Reading Road is just beyond the trees and sky line. The raised fields to the right with the large house are probably those which Robert Loder, in his *Farm Accounts, 1610–1620* called the 'hanging fields'.

LOWER BROADWAY AND ENGLEFIELD COTTAGE, at the turn of the twentieth century. The cottage is mid-sixteenth century, with seventeenth-century additions. The building which looks like a garage is Harwell's first fire station, which was demolished in 1973.

THE SAME VIEW, but much later, at the end of the 1930s.

THE BROADWAY again, pre-war.

JENNINGS LANE, c. 1935.

OLD COTTAGES IN THE WANTAGE ROAD, in the late 1940s. These sixteenth- or seventeenth-century cottages were demolished some years ago, and two bungalows occupy their former site. They were sited on the bend opposite the old Chequers pub, which has been made into a private house.

Park Corner, Harwell

THIS POSTCARD is entitled 'Park Corner, Harwell', and dates to the late 1920s. However, this area has so altered that it is hard to identify exactly where it was; possibly the junction of Wellshead and the Park, but if so all the buildings shown have now been demolished.

THE HOMESTEAD, High Street. Originally a farmhouse, which was built in 1797. This photograph dates to the late 1920s.

SNOW IN HARWELL, 16 April 1921. Poplar Cottages, the Poplars, in High Street. Now demolished, the site is a coal yard. They were early in date, possibly late sixteenth century.

MORE COTTAGES THAT HAVE GONE, these were higher up in the High Street, and the site is now Harwell Car Services Garage. Hard to believe that this is still the High Street. Taken in the late 1920s.

PILLAR HOUSE IN THE HIGH STREET, c. 1900. This house, built in 1852, immediately after the fire, was the home of two prominent painters of the nineteenth century. The first was John Bacon, a painter of domestic, genre and biblical scenes, a book illustrator, and later a fashionable portrait artist, who lived at Pillar House, from 1894 to 1899. The other was L. Leslie Brooke, who was equally prolific as a children's book illustrator, caricaturist, and a portrait, genre and landscape painter. He was resident in the house from 1899 to 1909. They both used the village and villagers for backgrounds and models. Brooke's most famous illustrated book was *Ring of Roses* in which Harwell houses, scenes and people appear. He was responsible, indirectly, for the first appearance of Beatrix Potter's books, for he endorsed her illustrations for Warne, the publisher. Another artist resident at Pillar House, this time during the 1960s, was Derek Southall, an abstract and landscape painter. During the 1930s and early 1940s, Miss Irene Clarke established her private school at Pillar House, where she taught young boys and girls up to the age of eleven years. She moved away from the house when it was sold in 1946, and continued the school at Osterley, Wellshead. The school was closed and Miss Clarke retired in 1966. The illustration dates to around 1900; the time that L. Leslie Brooke was living at Pillar House.

PRYORS SHOP, HIGH STREET; another house to be built almost immediately after the fire of 1852, and by Thomas James Pryor. The house is presumed to have replaced an earlier house and shop which it is thought was destroyed in the fire, because Pryor had been in business at Harwell since 1833. One of his sons, John Thomas Pryor, opened a shop in 1861, which was newly built at Didcot station. After the Second World War, the shop-front was remodelled by the Co-operative who had acquired the business. This view dates to around 1900.

THE HARWELL FEAST procession passes Pryor's old shop, Whit Monday, 1952. The Feast takes place on Whit Monday every other year. Like many such festivals it may be pagan in origin. Whit Monday has been an important day at Harwell for centuries. In earlier years it was a real feast, when hot 'sit-down' dinners were common. Before the First World War, the feast fell into disuse but was revived after 1918 by the British Legion. Today, it is an important biennial event.

THE ALMHOUSES IN HIGH STREET, C. 1900, these are on the left, while to the right is the old Crown pub (with steps) and Wilcote. The Crown, during the 1852 fire, was saved from destruction by a Mr Walters, who stayed on the thatched roof dowsing and throwing off burning embers as they fell. It was also in the Crown that the annual auction of the cherry crop took place; which was still on the trees. During the early 1950s, £1,600 was paid for a crop. The Crown is another pub that could not survive in the modern world; it has ceased to trade and is now a private nursing home, but the name has been retained – the Crown Nursing Home.

THE ALMHOUSES, the war memorial and the Crown in the later years of the late 1930s. The age of the motor!

Harwell Almshouses.

C 629.

THE GEERING ALMHOUSES, C. 1914. These were built by direction of Frances Geering through her will of 1723, to house six poor widows. If possible, they were to be born in Harwell but any widow fit for the object of charity would qualify. Lands were purchased to provide an income for maintenance of both widows and the almshouses. The rents were also to provide the widows on entering the almshouses with six new gowns and coats, and new ones every other year.

FURTHER UP HIGH STREET, outside Adnams Farmhouse, with Pryor's shop slightly lower down, c. 1929. It was in Adnams farmyard, then in the occupation of Mr Isaac Robey, that Harwell's great fire of 1852 broke out, at about 9 p.m. on a Saturday evening. That evening, there was a north-east wind blowing, and with the fire breaking out at the east end of the village, it quickly spread. Dry conditions made it even worse; and within an hour, thatched buildings and ricks of several adjoining farms were on fire. No less than five straw ricks were soon ablaze. A contemporary description said that the fire could be seen from Abingdon, and to an onlooker within the village, it appeared as it there was 'one unbroken light of fire' – a veritable wall of flame. Naturally, there was great panic, and everyone felt that the whole village would burn down. In all twenty-one dwelling houses and nine farm homesteads were destroyed. This is why the east side of the High Street consists of mainly post-1852 houses.

LOOKING UP HIGH STREET, with the barns of Middle Farm on the left, around the turn of the century.

THE UPPER PART OF HIGH STREET, with Grove Road, to the left, Yew Tree Cottage (a seventeenth-century house) and beyond the Old Brewery, early 1930s.

IN THE SAME PLACE. The Old Brewery in the distance, with Adnams Farm, and slightly lower down, is Druitt's Corner, in the late 1940s.

UPPER HIGH STREET, with Adnams, the Old Bakery and Druitt's old shop, around the end of the First World War.

LOOKING DOWN HIGH STREET in the early 1930s. On the immediate right is the shop run for decades by the two Miss Druitts – or Druitt's Corner as it was better known. They were familiar to generations of Harwell people. It was one of those old-fashioned general shops which sold everything – or so it seemed to those that used it. The house was late sixteenth century; and was demolished in 1963.

THE WHITE HART at the corner of Burr Street and High Street. A very old house of late sixteenth-century date, which was enlarged in the eighteenth and mid-nineteenth centuries. It has one particular feature 'a chamber over the entry'; this can be seen clearly. It was at first a bakery, then a pub, remaining so for the past three hundred and fifty years. In earlier centuries, it was a coaching inn, when the Wallingford–Wantage Turnpike road passed its doors; and to provide sufficient horses for the passing traveller it had plenty of stabling in the yard.

A VERY POPULAR SPOT FOR THE PHOTOGRAPHER: two more views, the first dates from around 1900, the other from the end of the First World War.

POMANDER HOUSE IN TOWNSEND, late 1940s. An early sixteenth-century house; its great cruck beams can just be seen.

KINGS FARM, early eighteenth century, at the corner of Townsend, late 1920s.

THE CHURCH OF ST MATTHEW, Church Lane, dates from around 1190, and was completed in its present form by 1310. The transepts, tower, nave arcades and low aisle date from the period 1190–1220; the chancel, 1290–1310; and the aisles heightened and porch built 1280–1320. The church is sited on rising ground next to Prince's Manor, and near to the Chilbrook, a nearby stream. Wellshed Farm was an early rectory.

THE OLD RECTORY, possibly sixteenth century in date but always a cold, damp house. It was demolished in the early 1960s. The photograph dates from around 1900.

CHURCH LANE in c. 1907. Locktons Farmhouse, an eighteenth-century house, is in the mid-distance.

CHURCH LANE, with Le Carillion, the church farmhouse, of mid-fifteenth century date. The photograph dates from c. 1905.

FURTHER DOWN CHURCH LANE in c. 1905. The wall of Le Carillion is on the farm-worker's left. The church is in the distance.

BROOKE FARMHOUSE, JENNINGS LANE, around 1900. The house dates from the late sixteenth century.

ANOTHER VIEW OF BROOKE FARM, possibly in the 1930s. The house has had some improvements: the ivy has gone, and there are new chimney pots on the nearest stack.

LOOKING UP BURR STREET towards the White Hart Corner. The house is Tudor Cottage, a late sixteenth-century house. Late 1940s.

BURR STREET; the Potters in the immediate foreground, and Tudor Cottage beyond. Taken in the late 1940s. Only forty years ago but what a difference those years have made. Today, instead of a quiet country lane, this is a busy, dangerous road, especially to those that live there; with a continual stream of motor cars.

DR RICHARD RICE, an old-fashioned country doctor, who commenced practice at Harwell in 1882, and retired in 1945 at the age of eighty-six years. He took over a practice which included Didcot, Chilton, Blewbury, and Upton, with even more patients farther afield at Wantage, Hanney, etc. He was a well-loved doctor, respected by all who knew him or were his patients. He was featured in more than one local book, such as *A Downland Corner* by the Revd Victor Whitchurch, or in *Travels Around our Village* by Eleanor Hayden. He was a churchwarden for twenty-one years and secretary of the parochial church council.

CHILDREN AT HARWELL SCHOOL, April 1909; Mr Charles Fuller, headmaster.

SURVIVORS FROM THE FIRST WORLD WAR who were photographed after the British Legion held a dinner to welcome home all village ex-servicemen.

The Moretons and Aston Tirrold

THE STAR PUB, formerly on the Didcot to Wallingford road, photographed sometime before the Second World War, and yet another pub to have closed – but when? It was commonly known as the Dirt House; and may have got this name because of its dirt floors. But a more romantic and preferred story is that in the nineteenth century, and before the advent of the lorry, gangs of drovers employed to move herds of animals, cattle, sheep and pigs to market, used to stay at the Star overnight, resting their animals in the fields around, and the pub got its name from their visits. The building is possibly seventeenth century in date; it was there in 1760, however, due to extensive dry rot it was demolished very recently.

HIGH STREET, South Moreton, in the late 1940s.

MANOR ROAD, South Moreton, again in the late 1940s. To the left is Forge Cottage, this is where Bud Finch, whose recent book, *Bud Finch Remembers,* describes his early life in the village, was born. It was once the blacksmith's shop. Further down the road is Manor Cottage and Manor Farm.

ST JOHN THE BAPTIST parish church, South Moreton. A church of great antiquity, dating back to the eleventh century. There are two parallel aisles and a vestry, the east end of one aisle forms the chancel. The aisles are divided by an Early English, five arched arcade. There is an early doorway, of the eleventh century, in the west wall. The south aisle was possibly added in the early thirteenth century. In 1849, the east wall was rebuilt, the old wooden tower pulled down, and the two bells hung in a new bellcote.

SPRING LANE at the end of the First World War. The Chequers Inn, seen here, is another pub that has closed.

ST MICHAEL'S, Aston Tirrold. Another very early church, which dates back to 1080. It is said to stand on a Saxon foundation; and there is an early doorway, reputedly of Saxon work. The building consists of flint with stone dressings, with a chancel, a nave of three bays, north aisle, south transept, south porch and an embattled tower. The church was remodelled in the thirteenth century; and the south transept and tower were added in the fourteenth.

THE RECTORY, Aston Tirrold, at the end of the First World War. The house was built in 1846 by a new incumbent, John Leigh Hoskyns, who later became Sir John on inheriting the family baronetcy in 1877. He pulled down the old parsonage house and barn, which were probably far more charming than the new building; this happened at Didcot, and probably Blewbury as well.

THE POST OFFICE, MORETON ROAD, C. 1918. The house next to the post office was also a shop in earlier times, and was run by the Maynard family.

THORPE STREET, C. 1931.

BLEWBURTON HOUSE OR HALL, C. 1918. This was a smaller (and earlier) house that was purchased and enlarged by a Major John Morris at the end of the nineteenth century. He was the first to start training horses at Upthorpe, and built the first stables.

ASTON TIRROLD CHURCH AND MANOR HOUSE. Side by side they stand, forming a trinity with the rectory, with squire and parson ruling the village and its people.

THE QUEEN ANNE MANOR HOUSE. A very beautiful house, with lines of perfect proportion. It was possibly built by a member of the Fuller family, and it is known that Joseph Fuller lived at the house in the early eighteenth century. But it is not known who actually built it – Richard Hatton, perhaps? The house was known as Aston Farm at that time. At the end of the nineteenth century, the Fullers sold the manor and house to John Kynaston Cross, who became lord of the manor. He became Chairman of the Wallingford Rural District Council; and it is after his middle name that Kynaston Road in Didcot is named.

ACKNOWLEDGEMENTS

No book can be written or in this case compiled without the aid of so many people; in my case I owe grateful thanks for the loan of postcards and photographs to:

Mr Don Farmborough ● Mrs Pansy Woodall ● Mr Roger Cambray
Mr Hector Cullen ● Willi Pereira of Isis Studios ● East Hagbourne School
Mr Thomas Dines ● *Oxford Times* Newspapers Ltd.

Grateful thanks for information to:

Dr Gordon and Mrs Una Walker ● Mrs Joanna Thomson ● Mrs Eileen Todorovic
Mrs Audrey Long ● Mr and Mrs Blond ● Mr Bernard Powell ● Miss Margaret Abbott

Lastly, two books that have proved invaluable: Northeast, P., *This Venerable Village: Some Notes on Blewbury, Harwell: a village for a thousand years,* and Whitwell, Stephen, *Tirrold and Upthorpe,* I thank the compilers.

HIGH STREET during the time of the First World War.